HANDBUCH DER ORIENTALISTIK

ZWEITE ABTEILUNG

III. BAND, 1. ABSCHNITT

HANDBUCH DER ORIENTALISTIK

Herausgegeben von B. SPULER
unter Mitarbeit von
H. FRANKE, J. GONDA, H. HAMMITZSCH, W. HELCK, B. HROUDA,
H. KÄHLER, J. E. VAN LOHUIZEN - DE LEEUW und F. VOS

ZWEITE ABTEILUNG

INDIEN

HERAUSGEGEBEN VON J. GONDA

DRITTER BAND

GESCHICHTE

ERSTER ABSCHNITT

HISTORY OF INDIAN LAW
(DHARMAŚĀSTRA)

LEIDEN/KÖLN
E. J. BRILL
1973

HISTORY OF INDIAN LAW
(DHARMAŚĀSTRA)

BY

J. DUNCAN M. DERRETT

LEIDEN/KÖLN
E. J. BRILL
1973

ISBN 90 04 03740 3

PRINTED IN BELGIUM

CONTENTS

ABBREVIATIONS

ABORI	Annals of the Bhandarkar Oriental Research Institute
AIR	All India Reporter
AOR	Annals of Oriental Research
A.P.	Andhra Pradesh
Bom.	Bombay
BSOAS	Bulletin of the School of Oriental and African Studies
C.S.S.H.	Comparative Studies in Society and History
HD	P.V. Kane, History of Dharmaśāstra
I.L.I.	Indian Law Institute
ISPP	Indian Studies Past and Present
IYBIA	Indian Yearbook of International Affairs
JAOS	Journal of the American Oriental Society
JAS	Journal of the Asiatic Society (Bengal)
JASB	Journal of the Asiatic Society of Bengal
RLSI	J.D.M. Derrett, Religion, Law and the State in India
S.C.	Supreme Court

CHAPTER ONE

THE PLACE OF HINDU LAW IN INDIA
THE DILEMMA OF MODERN REFORMERS

India, like many territories that once formed part of the colonial empires of Western powers, is a country having a general law (e.g. the law of contract, of civil wrongs, crime, insolvency, taxation, etc.) and what are called 'personal laws'. Hindus, Muslims, Christians, Parsis and Jews have each their own law applied to them in matters concerning the family, religion and religious organisation, by reason of the religion attributed, by law [1], to the individual litigant. The pattern (as distinct from de facto arrangements at, e.g., ports under Hindu Kings) was virtually introduced into India by Muslim Sultans in the tenth to thirteenth centuries, was recognised at once by Western traders as that in operation in the Ottoman Empire, with which they were familiar, and thus is, at the same time, a faithful representative of Asian traditional administrative methods and an affront to all presuppositions of modernity and progress. There is no emergent nation, newly independent, which does not yearn for legal unity; and India is no exception—saving the refusal of the great body of Muslims to yield and of the more bizarre features of the Shari'a law so far as it is still in force in India unamended. The implication of propaganda [2] for the reform of what is known as 'Muhammadan law', obviously overdue [3], is that the majority community (the Hindus), stimulated by a tiny minority of 'advanced' and educated Muslims, intend to force their ancient rivals to be 'civilised' and 'humane' [4]. This

---

1 Derrett, RSLI, chh. 1-2. See also below, p. 7, n. 1..

2 References at Derrett, RSLI, 537 n. 3. Surendra Prasad at AIR 1968 Journal 25-6; P. C. Jain at AIR 1969 Journal 136-9; T. P. Kelu Nambiar, 'The Damoclean "Talak" ', 1972 Kerala L. Times, Journal, 64-6. Note the sarcasm of the Śaṅkarācārya of Kamakoti Peetam (18 Aug. 1963) reported and discussed by T. S. Rama Rao (below, p. 6 n. 1), and of Subhadra Jha at his trans. of M. Winternitz, History of Indian Literature, III/2 (Delhi, 1967), 545.

3 See n. 2 above, also V. R. Krishna Iyer, 'Reform of Muslim matrimonial law', 1972 Kerala L. Times, Journal, 13-23.

4 Seminars conducted on this subject: Changes in Muslim Personal Law, a Symposium (Proceedings of the 26th Intern. Congr. of Orientalists, 1964, I, New Delhi, 1966); Islamic (Personal) Law in Modern India (New Delhi, 1972) (Bombay, I.L.I., 1972). See also D. E. Smith, South Asian Politics and Religion (Princeton, 1966); P. B. Gajendragadkar, Secularism (Bombay, 1971); also Family Law Reform in the Muslim World (Bombay, I.L.I., 1972).

conflict between the demands of reason and those of self-respect began in an acute form after 1955, when Hindu matrimonial law was reformed (see below); and it produced no tangible result by the time this chapter was written.

The personal laws conflicted. If a Christian died intestate no heir would be disqualified from succeeding to him (under the Indian Succession Act) merely because he was not a Christian when the succession opened; but if that non-Christian had died first his Christian relative could not have succeeded to him, because only actual converts (in the first generation) may retain a right of succession on intestacy notwithstanding their change of religion, which is normally a disqualification [1]. Such rules typify the archaic atmosphere of the personal laws. They may also be incompatible with each other. A Muslim might marry his paternal uncle's daughter, whereas practically no Hindu had the right to do this. Again a Muslim might divorce his wife by communication of a unilateral act of repudiation; a Hindu might not, generally, obtain a divorce except judically and upon proof of grounds for divorce. Even amongst Christians the laws of succession were not uniform. Art. 44 of the Constitution promised a code of civil law for all Indians, and towards the third quarter of the twentieth century this goal came closer into view. The history of this long and involved story commences for practical purposes in 1772.

In that year the East India Company's 'Presidency' at Calcutta, presided over by Warren Hastings, decided that its new-founded civil courts in Bihar, Orissa, and Bengal should administer Islamic law to Muslims and the law of the 'Shaster' (Dharmaśāstra) to Hindus when disputes arose upon any of a small number of topics, which included marriage, succession, religious institutions and matters of caste discipline [2]. Soon afterwards the King's court at Calcutta (called the Supreme Court) was created with a similar instruction by Parliament (the differences are no longer of interest) [3], and the East India Company gave its courts again, by a further Regulation [4], the jurisdiction to apply not English law, but Justice, Equity, and Good Conscience in all cases where neither the personal laws nor the Company's Regulations afforded a rule of decision. The British merchants thus shouldered the responsibility to administer, with a regularity unknown before their time, the corpora of ancient laws, and where these did not give the

[1] Caste Disabilities Removal Act, 21 of 1850.

[2] Plan for the Administration of Justice, 15 Aug. 1772. See Derrett, RSLI, 232 n. 2.

[3] Derrett, ibid., 236.

[4] Derrett at J. N. D. Anderson, ed., Changing Law in Developing Countries (London, 1963), 133.

answer the (at first) amateur judge was to turn to a developed system of law, consistently with natural justice.

In course of time the influence of English law, being the only system regularly consulted under the heading of Justice, Equity, and Good Conscience, began to be felt heavily [1]. Bengal, Bihar, and Orissa on the one hand, and the Presidencies of Madras and Bombay on the other, experienced the growth, independently, of a kind of Anglo-Indian law, administered by courts which regarded themselves as virtually bound by precedent, a thing unknown before the British came. The system of appeals, whereby the Privy Council in London was the highest court of appeal, and settled finally the law for, at least, a large area with every one of the very many decisions it arrived at, made the principle *stare decisis* much more than a mere maxim. In the French and Portuguese territories the mother country exercised similar supervision, but the relation between indigenous law and custom and the court-law was somewhat more intimate, though there were important technical differences which extend beyond our present scope [2]. In British India the native 'laws' began to be researched into, and to obtain a rigidity which their professors could never have expected.

It is true that scope for development, for (in effect) judicial legislation, remained. But it could only be slow, hesitant, and partial. Radical reforms, taking account of visible social change, could not be attained without the aid of statutes. One may take for example the challenges effected by the gradual emancipation of women as, contrary to the unanimous assertion of the śāstras that 'a woman is never fit for independence', they took, in the twentieth century, to education and employment; and those arising from the liberalising of family law as individual males sought to earn and to make their own careers in semi-separation from the families into which they were born [3]. Yet statutes, representing the aspirations of an educated and cosmopolitan segment of society could not be expected to *effect* any reform unaided by a corresponding change throughout all elements of the public.

About eighty per cent of Indians were Hindus. To them the Hindu law applied. The Dharmaśāstra never mentioned mlecchas (non-Hindus) except in disparaging terms and excluded them entirely from its scope; it offered

---

1 See p. 2, n. 4, also Manjhoori v. Akal (1913) 17 Calcutta Weekly Notes 889, 916.

2 Bibliographies on Franco- and Luso-Hindu Law see Derrett, 'The Indian Subcontinent...' (biblio. below), pp. 40-42. On the law of the former French possessions see also S. C. Jain, 'French legal system in Pondicherry', J.I.L.I., 12 (1971), 573-608; J. Minattur at J.I.L.I., 13 (1971), 436-42.

3 Derrett, RSLI, ch. 12.

no resistance to the importation and enforcement of foreign religious or customary laws, and never purported to be a territorial law in the modern Western sense. The Hindu law thus spoke only to, and was concerned exclusively with Hindus, and conversion from Hinduism to another religion was the only way in which the jurisdiction acquired at an individual's birth could be escaped [1]. In course of time topics of law other than those listed by Warren Hastings became the objects of legislative codification, and Anglo-Indian statute law (towards which the śāstra and its professors adopted no particular attitude) occupied the fields of procedure, criminal law, contract, transfer of property, easements, limitation of actions, and many other necessary areas of law [2]. There were contexts in which the general law (e.g. regarding testamentary succession) and the personal laws touched, and there was a gradual, and incomplete, assimilation in course of time between the two, in which each made concessions in the interests of a workable compromise.

The third quarter of the twentieth century saw Hindu law supreme in the following fields, provided that the person or persons concerning whose rights the litigation had arisen had not put himself outside the personal law by marrying in a secular form, or, in the French possessions, by 'renouncing' the law of his religion: legitimacy, guardianship, adoption, marriage, matrimonial causes and divorce, the joint family and its dealings with strangers, succession (testamentary and intestate), religious endowments, dāmdupat (alterum tantum), and impartible estates. The Hindu law of preemption has been merged within the various State statutes on the subject. Muslims were similarly placed in that in the listed topics, which came to include items which were not expressly mentioned in the list, namely preemption [3], gifts and other transfers of property, and trusts for the benefit of issue, the rules discernable from the Qur'an and the Sunna were administered (in a mode which came to be known as Anglo-Muhammadan law) [4] with the appropriate differences between the Sunni and Shi'i schools. For Jews, Christians and Parsis no such arrangement was made, but it seems that under Justice, Equity, and Good Conscience the Jewish law, [5] and Canon

---

[1] The Anglo-Hindu law admitted the right of persons to become Hindus by conversion (Derrett, Introduction to Modern Hindu law, Bombay, 1963, § 17) and it was thought possible to be a member of a Hindu joint family though a Christian by religion (Derrett at Madras Law Journal, 1970, pt. 2, Journal, 1-8).

[2] W. Stokes, The Anglo-Indian Codes (Oxford, 1887-8); Supplements (Oxford, 1889, 1891).

[3] Not admitted in Madras, see Derrett cited at p. 2, n. 4. above, p. 142, n. 4.

[4] R. K. Wilson, A Digest of Anglo-Muhammadan Law[5] (Calcutta/Simla, 1921).

[5] Derrett, cited at p. 3, n. 2. above, p. 20.

law [1] were consulted respectively (this remains true in contexts other than those covered by general statutes); while Parsi customs were discovered and to some extent codified and provision was made for the administration of certain aspects of Parsi law (notably matrimonial disputes and the law of succession on intestacy) by statutes [2].

A weakness of both Hindu and Islamic law was the want of a centrally organised means of reviewing their content and suitability. Jewish law is conversant with the concept of majority decision: this never existed in Hindu law and its function in Islamic law has been meagre and controversial. The Indian Law Commission, when set up, and again re-created by the central legislature from the middle of the nineteenth century [3], had, from time to time, competence to recommend changes, but the personal laws have in fact long resisted this instrument. The Hindu law's reform was mooted in the 1920's and became an active project by 1941. It went through stages (known as the 'Hindu Code' controversy) [4] until 1955-6 when the four main statutes of 'modern Hindu law' were passed [5]. They impinged heavily on all parts of the personal law, but did not, in several areas, abrogate the Anglo-Hindu law, which was the dharmaśāstra as developed by the Anglo-Indian administration. The reforms were subsequently introduced into the former French possessions, saving the status of the 'renouncers' [6]. The reform of Islamic law was commenced shortly before the Second World War, firstly by the extension of the Muslim personal law to many groups who professed to be orthodox in all but the customary law which they derived from their Hindu past [7], and secondly by the substantial liberalising of the marriage law in the Dissolution of Muslim Marriages Act [8]. The further reform of Islamic law, especially in view of initiatives taken in that direction in Pakistan, was repeatedly urged by Hindus after the Hindu law was itself reformed [9], and as an attempt to put into effect

[1] Ibid., p. 21; but see also Derrett, 'Native Converts' Marriage Dissolution Act, 1866: Should it be Abolished?', Bombay Law Reporter, 74, Journal (1972), 16-23. See also Lakshmi Sanyal v. Sachit, AIR 1972 S.C. 2667.

[2] Derrett, cited at p. 3, n. 2 above, pp. 21-2, esp. P. K. Irani in J. N. D. Anderson, ed., Family Laws in Asia and Africa (London, 1968), 273-300. The system is illustrated by Merchant v. Merchant AIR 1970 Bom. 341.

[3] G. C. Rankin, Background to Indian Law (Cambridge, 1946).

[4] Derrett, Hindu Law Past and Present (Calcutta, 1957). Hindu Law Reform: A Short Introduction ((Delhi), Publication Div., Min. of Information and Broadcasting, Govt. of India, (1955)).

[5] To be seen in Mulla, and Derrett, Introduction to Modern Hindu Law (cited above).

[6] See S. C. Jain, cited at p. 3, n. 2 above.

[7] Muslim Personal Law (Shariat) Application Act, 26 of 1937. Derrett, RSLI, 520-9.

[8] Act 8 of 1939.

[9] P. 1, n. 2,4.

Art. 44 of the Constitution, the intention behind which formed the subject of lively debates in the decade from 1960 [1]. Conservative Muslims view the scheme with antagonism, and remain unmoved by the wholesale reform of the controversial areas of Islamic law in countries with predominantly Muslim populations. For the pure Islamic law, Sunni and Shi'i the reader is referred to the work of O. Spies and E. Pritsch in the Handbuch der Orientalistik [2].

This chapter concerns the indigenous law of India, which is not Christian, Jewish, Parsi, or Muslim. It is Hindu law, partaking from its inception of a uniquely Indian character. Important as they are for the day-to-day administration, the personal laws of communities that entered India or converted from Hinduism are non-typical of India. Our attention will now be concentrated on the lessons to be learnt from the history of Hindu law. The twentieth century saw the maturing of a process which began in 1772, in which India as a congeries of legally self-sufficient communities and sects congealed into a state unitary in law as it was unitary in political self-government. If Hindu law was to be abolished to make way for a Code of family law for all communities the legislators required an academic as well as a practical, an objective as well as subjective notion of what they were replacing. In the 1970's Hindu law was supposed to be a problem no more; the excitement its reform had aroused had receded. Constitutional law, fiscal law, administrative, corporation and criminal law received attention. Other problems cried out for solution, and the personal law of the majority had been attended to by Parliament by 1956. The dilemma presented by the portion dealing with the joint family, which the public have by no means digested in its semi-reformed condition, retained seeds of still more anxiety to which legislators would be alert. The enactment, for example, of an adoption law for all Indians would involve the abolition of the Hindu law of adoption. Yet Hindus would for long adopt in the old form and for the old motives and with the old limitations (only sons would be adopted, and there would be no more than one adoptee at a time, to continue the line). The chaotic result would reach its climax (as judicial arrears persist) only when final appeals have been heard years after the disputed adoptions. Similarly a new divorce law must contend with the engrained habit of using litigation not so much to obtain justice as to harass 'enemies'. Meanwhile,

---

[1] P. 1, nn. 3-4 above, also articles in J. Constitutional and Parliamentary Studies, 3/3 (1969). T. S. Rama Rao, 'Codification and Unification of Indian Law,' Unidroit (Rome), 1962, 111-130. (publ. 1963).

[2] Klassisches Islamisches Recht, Hb. d. Orientalistik, Ergänzungsband III (Leiden/Köln, 1964).

the claim that the Hindu law defied the Constitution's promise of equality or non-discrimination, and should be modified (judicially) accordingly has been uniformly rejected by the courts [1].

A virtue of the ancient system, retained in its Anglo-Hindu guise, was that it left ample room for India's great diversity of viewpoints, traditions, and behaviour-patterns; whereas Parliament's formal assumption of a social unity which has not yet appeared has, in practice, created more problems than it solved, since judicial decisions from the Punjab will be cited in Kerala, and those from Bombay have persuasive authority in Bengal.

---

1 See G. Sambireddy v. G. Jayamma (1972) 1 Andhra Weekly Reporter 294 (Full Bench) and cases therein cited; also the plea (note the date!) of R. S. Venkatachari (to modify the Schedule to the Hindu Succession Act, 1956) at Madras Law Journal, 1972, vol. 2, Journal, 34-36.

CHAPTER TWO

THE CORPUS IURIS OF HINDU LAW IN 1772

a) *The extent of the subject-matter*

The Dharmaśāstra (here called 'the śāstra') is the Indian 'science of righteousness'. Its literary character and history are dealt with by the same writer in J. Gonda's History of Indian Literature. Its authoritative texts stemmed from well before our era, continuing to be composed, and revised in various forms for two thousand years. It covered a very large field of norms. In practical (secular) contexts it was supplemented by the customs of guild members, such as those of smiths, physicians, architects, and the commercial law operating between inter-regional and even inter-national merchants and money-lenders. Of these customs the authors and jurists (śāstrīs) were aware, but they were not in a position to come to know these professional matters in detail, nor could they produce a generalisation or abstraction which would be of any utility. Books of precedents [1] show us the shape of the law actually operating in such contexts. With its emphasis on the supersensory or occult significance attributed by the public to ritual acts and also to actions of a seemingly purely social or economic import, it took care, in principle and often in considerable but never exhaustive detail, of every phase of life from antenatal existence to cremation, prescribing and even describing ceremonies to propitiate evil forces likely to hinder a propitious state or prosperous rebirth. It is evident from this that the śāstra went far further than law in the modern western sense; it harmoniously embraced moral, social, intellectual, spiritual, and psychiatric problems along with those that would appear to us to be entirely legal. Even legal problems in an Indian environment were, as they still are, except in the business-world of the greater towns, only parts in a complex network of relationships in which individuals and their troubles function only within the group; inter-personal relations often figuring as an aspect of inter-group relations, the psychological value of abstracting and objectivising relationships and transactions by emphasising their occult contextuality is obvious. In our more homogeneous and individualistic world the superficial signific-

[1] Lekhapaddhati (Baroda, 1925) (see Derrett, RSLI, index, s.v.); Lokaprakāśa; Vidyāpati's Likhanāvalī (see B. Bhattacharya, ISPP 8, 1966-7, 251-7; S. L. Jha, JAS, 10, 1968, 46-8).

ance of transactions seems to exhaust their meaning, and persons left to bear the burden of their lives alone sense the possibility of an occult relationship between desire and fulfilment, without an effective education in 'otherworldly' perception to which the ancient, and particularly the Asian world was habituated. At first glance an Asian system of law appears not merely superstitious, but tediously footling; if scholars seek to understand the structure which binds the whole they may be rewarded.

The range of topics committed to the śāstra can be made out rapidly if we consult the scope of Lakṣmīdhara's Kṛtya-kalpataru (11th-12th cent.). The Book of Studentship (Brahmacāri-kāṇḍa) deals with definitions, including that of dharma; the purifying and consecrating ceremonies called saṃskāras starting from conception until tonsure, then initiation (upanayana) for boys of the three higher varṇas (Brahmins, Kṣatriyas, Vaiśyas); the duties of a student, the teacher-pupil relationship; Vedic instruction; perpetual studentship and the normal 'graduation' (entry into the transitional status of a snātaka). The Book of the Householder (Gṛhastha-kāṇḍa) deals with marriage, the rights and duties of the householder, supersession (the euphemistic and 'righteous' re-structuring of customary polygyny); offerings in fire (agnihotra); occupations befitting a Brahmin and other castes, including Śūdras (the lowest Hindu varṇa); observances of daily life, avoidance of causes of sin, including inter-caste sexual union; the need to beget sons who will pay their father's debts and save him from hell. The Book of Times deals with the moments for the householder's daily religious ceremonies. Śrāddha is the ceremony done to secure a deceased member's place in the world of ancestors, and also to propitiate ancestors. The Book of Śrāddhas deals with all aspects and variations of that ceremony. The Book of Gifts (Dāna-kāṇḍa) deals with religious and charitable donations having unseen rewards, including the dedication of wells and tanks for the public's use. The Book of Consecrations (Pratiṣṭhā-kāṇḍa) deals with pilgrimages, listing the famous resorts throughout India. The Book of Vows (Vrata-kāṇḍa) deals with voluntary vows for one's own, or another's merit. The topic of penance is missing from the Kṛtya-kalpataru but it is dealt with in other great digests. Penances exist to cleanse the sinner and enable him to be readmitted to commensality and other caste privileges, and also counteract the supposed effect of sins in past lives. Penance was necessary for the readmission of people who had undergone unusual experiences as well as criminals or breakers of the moral order. The system was fully operational in the early nineteenth century and gradually withdrew during the latter part of that and the earlier part of the next century. The reconciling of the smṛtis which formed the basic texts on this subject was an exceptionally intricate task—Manu himself provided alternatives, which made little sense if they were available to any one community in any one area.

Lakṣmīdhara's Śuddhi-kāṇḍa (Book of Purifications) deals with hygienic and ritual purification of persons and things. The Book of Dharma of Kings (Rāja-dharma-kāṇḍa) deals with what it is prudent for a king to do and with the rituals he must observe. Political science and revenue are touched upon vaguely: these come within the scope of the arthaśāstra (the science of ways and means), and, understandably, by the sixteenth and seventeenth centuries digest-compilers in dharmaśāstra borrow from the Kāmandakīya and similar arthaśāstra material. The Vyavahāra-kāṇḍa which logically figures here, may be left for consideration in more detail below. The Book of Propitiations (Śānti-kāṇḍa) deals with rites deemed needful to propitiate deities, avert malign influences of stars and portents, etc. The Book of 'Release' (Mokṣa-kāṇḍa), the last book, deals with the steps necessary for release from the circle of rebirth, and with identification with Brahma; spiritual concentration to prepare the soul's fitness to journey after death; and the stages of life of the forest hermit, the renunciate or ascetic (sannyāsī). With this book all aspects of life in the four varṇas and four stages of life (āśramas) have been covered, and the lack of a book on penance is to be attributed to some mishap in transmission. The topic of karma-vipāka, the 'burning out' of the remnants of evil karma accumulated due to unexpiated sins in this or previous lives can form a self-contained chapter of the śāstra, as in the Madanamahārṇava of Viśveśvara-bhaṭṭa (14th cent.).

What precedes serves to place the Vyavahāra-kāṇḍa (the 'litigation' section) in its perspective—the duty of the King to give justice lies within the whole concept of a dharmic ideal: and all the aids of reasoning and deduction were applied by the jurists to make the traditional texts, the primary sources, and their more ancient widely-accepted glosses, viable in daily life wherever dharmic principles were accepted, which occurred wherever Hindu culture, based on the Vedas, came to dominate. It is worth remembering that Jainas, and, in South India, sects drawing their Āryan cultural inspiration from Jaina missionary endeavour in their midst, developed and retained a corpus of dharma of their own, with its vyavahāra and its ācāra portions recognisably analogous to the Hindu dharma-śāstra: the implications of which remain to be worked out [1].

[1] The debt owed by Tamil didactic works (e.g. Peruvāyin Muḷḷiyār's Āsārak kōvai, printed in the Padiṉeṉ kīḻkkaṇakku) to Sanskrit sources cannot yet be estimated. N. Subrahmanian, Śaṅgam Polity (N.T., A.P.H., 1966). S. Singaravelu, Social Life of the Tamils (Kuala Lumpur, 1966). N. Muguresa Mudaliar, 'Polity in Tirukkural', AOR, 22 (= separately published, University of Madras, 1968). For Jainas see C. R. Jain, Jaina Law (Madras, 1926); D. C. Jain, 'Jain

Lakṣmīdhara's Vyavahāra-kāṇḍa (Book of Civil Laws) covers both procedural and adjectival law, the vyavahāra-mātṛkā and the vyavahāra-padas (topics of litigation). It commences with a description of vyavahāra and a discussion of local, caste, guild, and family customs. He proceeds to describe the administration of law: the judge, assessors, procedure, evidence, oaths, documentary proof, decrees, forgeries, possession as a title, inference, ordeals, the decision and judgment, appeals. He then moves to the eighteen topics or titles of litigation. The number 18 remained a formal constant [1] throughout the history of the śāstra, but by Lakṣmīdhara's time it had been stretched to nineteen with a miscellaneous section! Lakṣmīdhara arranges the topics as follows: (1) debt, (2) deposit, (3) sales by persons others than the owners, (4) joint enterprises, (5) non-delivery of gifts, (6) aspects of master and servant relations, misbehaviour of dependants, and slavery; (7) non-payment of wages, (8) disputes between herdsmen and the owner of cattle, (9) breach of undertakings between members of groups, e.g. breach of by-laws, (10) withdrawal from purchases, (11) boundary disputes, (12) verbal assault, e.g. abuse, (13) physical assault, (14) theft, (15) mayhem (sāhasa), (16) rape and improper relations between the sexes, (17) relations between husband and wife, conjugal duties and loyalty, (18) division of family property (dāya-vibhāga), including adoption and descent and distribution, the heaviest of the legal topics, (19) gambling and miscellaneous topics, including conflicts between legal acts, buried treasure and the duties of the mixed castes, i.e. supposed descendants of unions between parents of different varṇas. That descendants of miscogeny might form a caste, and develop laws and customs of their own, is reported as a fact in modern Nepal, and has a very close parallel in the Basters of Namibia, whose self-given laws illustrate the influence of tradition, a mixed heredity, and the peculiar conditions of socially isolated living [2]. The elaborate superstructure raised by the śāstrīs, which has every appearance of being unrealistic, thus stood upon a practical foundation.

The Smṛti-candrikā of Devaṇṇa-bhaṭṭa (thirteenth cent.) introduces the topic of joint enterprises (e.g. partnership) after (3) and places (5) immediately next. Topic (3) is then placed after (7), which must have seemed more

---

jurisprudence', Intern. J. of Legal Res. 2 (1967), 137-46; R. Williams, Jaina Yoga (London, 1963). For the history of the application of 'Hindu Law' to Jainas subject to their protests see Comm. of Wealth Tax v. Champa Kumari AIR 1972 S.C. 2119 and the references there cited. For Buddhist law see A. S. Altekar, 'Sanskrit literature in Tibet', ABORI, 35 (1954), 63.

[1] O. Stein, 'The numeral 18', Poona Orientalist 1 (1936), 1-37.

[2] W. P. Carstens, The Social Structure of a Cape Coloured Reserve (Cape Town, 1966). Union of S. Africa: Report of the Reheboth Commission (U.G. 41-'26) (Cape Town, 1927).

logical. The next topic is not Lakṣmīdhara's (8) but a new one called 'non-delivery of things sold'. No. (11) is rearranged as 'disputes arising out of agricultural land', as it includes irrigation and similar problems. Nos. (12) and (13) are postponed to (17) and (18). It is arguable whether this is a more intelligible order. Lakṣmīdhara's no. (6) is omitted, but the subject-matter of (6) and (8) is merged under the heading 'failure to pay wages'. Nīlakaṇṭha in his Vyavahāra-mayūkha alters the order still further (17th cent.) placing no. (1) as the nineteenth topic—the arrangement under eighteen headings is abandoned. Nīlakaṇṭha and his predecessor (author of the Madana-ratna-pradīpa) include in their treatment of dāya (no. 18 above) a profound study of property in the abstract. Nīlakaṇṭha also adds several crimes, including that of deciding a case wrongly as a judge, and considers the topic of fines, and the king's penance for levying fines unjustly! The Vīramitrodaya of Mitra-miśra (17th cent.) introduces no further topics by way of changing the principal headings. It is of interest that leases of land do not appear even as a sub-topic, until Pratāpa-rudra's Sarasvatī-vilāsa (16th cent.), and the precedent is not followed [1]. Preemption fades from the advanced śāstric treatises, into which it makes fitful appearances, reemerging in an Islamised guise in the late eighteenth century [2]. These instances show the delicacy of the relationship between the śāstra and practical affairs from century to century. Where high variability from district to district would impair the majestic universality and detachment affected by the śāstric texts, even the most important topic was at risk: and in the later medieval period systematic study of fiscal problems and other problems relating to immoveable property, though it must have gone on, is not evidenced amongst the śāstras—so that failure on the part of the dharmaśāstra did not necessarily encourage the emergence of an alternative. The great rarity of arthasāstra manuscripts, and the paucity of commentaries upon the Kauṭilīya Artha-śāstra, indicate that, at least as a scholastic medium, that śāstra did not take up the slack.

b) *The enforcement of rules*

Śāstric rules were not regularly enforced by legal process as we understand it. Even where the royal judge gave a final decision in a matter which we should identify as litigation, the execution of the decree was left to the successful party, and the most the system did to help him was to insist upon the defendant's giving security for submission to the decree, and to fine the un-

---

1 Derrett, 'Kuttā', BSOAS, 21 (1958), 61-81.

2 Derrett, RSLI, 161 n. 5.

successful party for sustaining a false case. Apart from the adversary procedure, in which the judge assisted in the ascertainment of truth, the king (as the śāstra paints him) originally reserved to himself numerous duties of correcting, and visiting the varṇas and āsramas. Even at the end of the development of the basic sources of the śāstra the king was expected to reserve a number of matters of business within his scope, called prakīrṇaka. His duty to protect the public included the duty of giving justice, but this was visualised more as a matter of putting an end to serious disputes between social units, ostensibly figuring as grievances of individuals, than giving law or upholding justice in its entirety.

Originally his authority was not needed for the internal self-government of each unit: excommunication, outcasting, was the ultimate penalty and it was plainly more than sufficient as long as each village withheld village services (e.g. the ministrations of the potter and the barber) from those who had been excommunicated. Later the king's duty was said to include supervision of all penalties, including those inflicted by caste tribunals. Before an offender paid his fine or performed his penance and was readmitted to caste privileges the king's permission was sought. It was plain that both a secular and a spiritual and social penalty were required in pre-British times before an individual was clean again, unless the secular penalty operated also as a penance (which would be the case if it were a death penalty which left, of course, no room for readmission to caste). The peculiar case of the self-confessed thief of gold, whose personal punishment at the hands of the ruler acted as a penance, shows how closely connected, in ancient times, were the ideas of penalty and penance. Penalty was thought of as a deterrent; penance was required for reintegration.

Many disputes could not be brought by the aggrieved parties, but were promoted suo motu as the outcome of the king's officers' enquiries, including espionage [1]. Pupils could not with propriety bring actions against their teachers, nor wives against their husbands nor sons against their fathers [2]. but the substance of such disputes would come within the king's jurisdiction on the basis of what would, in our Canon law, be called 'instance' procedure. Breach of ritual requirements would be punished by the village, or by a committee of Brahmins, and in this way caste discipline was kept up until well into the British period, and even thereafter to a limited degree [3]. It was the decadence of the moral and social aspects of enforcement of

---

1 Kane, HD, III, 251-7.

2 See last note, also L. Rocher, 'The theory of matrimonial causes according to the Dharmaśāstra', in J. N. D. Anderson, ed., Family Law in Asia and Africa (cited above), 90-117.

3 Derrett, RLSI, 472-7. Kane, HD, III, 935-8.

the śāstra which paved the way for the characteristic dichotomy between traditional, 'true' Hindu law and the court-law, which, well into the twentieth century, was regarded as a kind of gamble. The presentation of false cases, and harassment through litigation, the overloading of the courts with vast arrears, and the procedural skill of advocates which drew out otherwise simple cases, turned the adventure of litigation into an unduly prolonged distraction [1]. Yet is it known that even experienced litigants by no means became well versed in legislation, much of which hardly filtered down to the village level, in spite of the existence of certain legal textbooks in regional languages.

Many śāstric rules could not be enforced at all, operating solely through the conscience or habitual choice. When afflicted with incurable disease or an inexplicable run of misfortunes, the conservative Hindu might come to 'realise' that his undharmic living was responsible (e.g. his having lived with a widow as man and wife, permitted by statute since 1850 but still anathema to the orthodox). And then ceremonies were provided to avert the evil omen and counteract the effects of the demerit which had accumulated. On the positive side society knew well that in 1955 polygamy had been prohibited (Hindu Marriage Act, sec. 5(*i*)), but still the śāstra, and the Anglo-Hindu law, had permitted plural marriages of males, and therefore bigamous marriages after 1955 were tolerated, and, at the formal level, condoned with the aid of mere legalistic technicalities [2]. The place of law was thus, like many features of Hindu life, a mixed one, and dual attitudes obtained. The norm was stated, imperfect arrangements were made to enforce it, and these arrangements were treated flexibly and unpredictably.

c) *The extent of the literature, and an account of selected principal works*

Kane's list of authors [3] enables us to estimate that approximately two thousand writers contributed to the literature, not including those anonym-

---

[1] Law Commission of India. Fourteenth Report (Reform of Judicial Administration), 2 vols. (Delhi, 1958). V. D. Mahajan, Chief Justice Gajendragadkar (Delhi, 1966), passim. Chief Justice K. S. Hegde at 1972 Kerala L. Times, Journal, 51, 'Few months ago, I had to decide a case from this High Court, which had taken 22 years for reaching a final decision ... So far as High Courts are concerned, they are burdened with unnecessary litigation. Some of these are quite frivolous. I know of a High Court where even income-tax cases are pending for half-a-dozen years or more. In one particular High Court, there is a pendency of as many as 85,000 cases, including about 12,000 income tax references'.

[2] Derrett, Critique of Modern Hindu Law (Bombay, 1970), 296-301.

[3] An appendix to Kane, HD, I.

ous authors of epics and purāṇas which ultimately swelled the collections of medieval jurists. Some additional authors will no doubt appear in time. Well over two thousand works are known, some of them of immense size, such as the Ṭoḍarānanda, in 80,000 ślokas. Further minor works will be traced. Of the whole a considerable quantity of the most significant portions has been published, but the scope for publication remains far larger than the funds or interest available. Much publishing of texts was due to the public spirit and piety of State Durbars, e.g. those of Baroda and Bikaner, putting their rich libraries to good use. More would have been done in this direction, even by the Union government or its predecessor [1], had the real function and significance of the śāstra been known.

Any scholar (in practice a Brahmin necessarily) who had completed his preliminary Vedic studies, and knew the basic texts by heart, such as the Gautama-dharma-sūtra, the Manu-smṛti, and the Yājñavalkya-smṛti, could, after studying with one or more specialists in the śāstra, make a profound study of any section or sections, gathering all the surviving basic texts (sūtras and smṛtis, with excerpts from purāṇas) and, summarising the opinions of his more accessible predecessors, make an original summary of the law, ironing out controversies and discrepancies as he went along. In this way texts of doubtful provenance but useful information became generally known, and some texts which could not be reconciled by any use of imagination fell out of circulation. Variant readings accumulated, and were eliminated from commentaries and digests, to survive however in bare texts—and the reverse also occurred. Works partaking ostensibly of the character of commentaries really served as digests, of which Aparārka's commentary on the Yājñavalkya-smṛti is the most notable example.

The very earliest commentary cannot be selected, as chronology is uncertain. Bhāruci's Vivaraṇa on the Manu-smṛti, Viśvarūpa's Bāla-krīḍā on the Yājñavalkya-smṛti, and Maskarī's bhāṣya on the Gautama-dharma-sūtra form the earliest group, all of which must have been composed before the end of the seventh century. The latest productions in the śāstra belong to the third to the fifth decade of the nineteenth century. The jargon of jurists remained (barring some fitful influence from the navya-nyāya from the sixteenth century onwards) remarkably stable from the beginning to the end of the literature. One might, in about 1850, use works from the seventh to the eighteenth centuries without sensing incongruity or incoherence, just as in the field of Romano-canonical studies authors of the eighteenth century in Europe utilised their predecessors from Azo to Zasius.

1 The Ministry of Education financed the publication of the Viṣṇusmṛti by V. Krishnamacharya from the Adyar Library (Theosophical Soc.) in 1964 Also Manu from Bombay (1972-).

In legal and social contexts certain śāstric works assumed prominence as a result of the revival of Hindu legal studies after the establishment of British rule. Vijñāneśvara's Mitākṣarā is a commentary on the Yājñavalkya-smṛti famous for its rapid and efficient reconciliation of conflicting smṛtis; in the realm of marriage and inheritance it acquired authority far beyond the Deccan whence it emanated. Jimūtavāhana's Dāyabhāga was an independent treatise written to prove a theory about the relationship between the right to succeed and the duty to provide spiritual benefit for the deceased. Both works, in so far as they dealt with inheritance, were translated by Colebrooke and formed basic texts for the courts. Jagannātha's Vivādabhaṅgārṇava, written in the last decade of the eighteenth century to serve the needs of Anglo-Indian courts, is an encyclopedia better suited to the legal historian than the judge. The Smṛticandrikā of Devaṇṇabhaṭṭa and the Sarasvatīvilāsa, the latter translated much sooner than the former, became authorities in the Eastern part of the Peninsula. Nīlakaṇṭha's Vyavahāra-mayūkha, apart from the other portions of his treatise, became a standard authority in the Bombay Presidency. It was not a commentary, but an independent treatment in which, as in Jīmūtavāhana's case, smṛti texts appeared as the authorities for the law being taught by the author. In the realm of adoption Nanda-paṇḍita's Dattaka-mīmāṃsā was often consulted, though its author's theoretical skill did not always find translation into law; and Kubera's Dattaka-candrikā was also an authoritative work on the same topic, wrongly suspected of being spurious. On the borders of Bengal, the region known as Mithilā produced a large number of jurists known for their disagreements with their colleagues in Bengal, the 'Easterners'. Of Maithila jurists Caṇḍeśvara and Vācaspati-miśra are best known, both being essentially compilers of smṛtis with a running commentary connecting and explaining them. On the law of the so-called Benares school, i.e. the central body of śāstric writers not propounding views which were subsequently adopted in specific regions, Mitra-miśra, author of two works called Vīramitrodaya, is regarded as a prime authority. Mādhava's commentary on the Parāśara-smṛti (14th cent.) became a leading legal treatise for the Deccan and South India, and was occasionally utilised in Anglo-Hindu law. On the whole the British preferred to utilise ancient digests and commentaries rather than the bare text of smṛti, for the familiar question, whether a scriptural text had been 'received' in any jurisdiction, was present to the Privy Council's mind; there are, however, instances where the wisdom of the jurists was doubted and the smṛti text, in its obvious meaning, was applied [1].

[1] Derrett, RLSI, 299 n. 5.

Numerous works of importance were rarely cited because no translations were available until recently. The heroic pioneering activity of J. R. Gharpure in publishing texts and translations started a little too late. The Madana-ratna-pradīpa, edited by Kane etc. (in part), appeared much too late to influence the trend of case-law, already well established on the footing of stare decisis. Varadarāja made little impact, though a late nineteenth century translation was utilised [1]. An advocate in Bombay had the enterprise to resurrect the vast Pṛthvīcandrodaya, editing a part of it and citing another in litigation [2], but the publication of the greater part of this vast and exemplary work awaits the re-accumulations of funds, and editorial energy. Chance factors still determine what is available for study, as they did, tragically, during the formative period of Anglo-Hindu law.

Kauṭilya's Arthaśāstra, rediscovered in about 1909, has been occasionally cited in judgments, though it supplies no more than tentative evidence of what must have been customary somewhere, appealing to 'Kauṭilya' as seeming practical and politic. A work of the Ārya Samāj has actually been cited in litigation, and several marginal and even primarily ritual works [3].

---

[1] By A. C. Burnell (Mangalore, 1872).

[2] A. v. B. (1952) 54 Bombay Law Reporter 725; J. H. Dave at (1953) Bombay Law Reporter, Journal, 25.

[3] Derrett, Critique (cited above), 415-16. A good example of the unpredictability of the corpus of Hindu works from which the Anglo-Indian courts would select their authorities arises in Kandasami v. Doraisami (1880) Indian Law Rep. 2 Madras 317, at 325. The 'Dāyarahasya' was apparently the Dāyabhāgaviveka of Rāmanātha, a commentary on Jīmūtavāhana's Dāyabhāga, composed in 1657 and never translated. A judicial decision could give a spurious text validity: Yama on adoption in Saminatha v. Vageesan (1940) Mad. 98 (Patanjali Sastri, J.).

CHAPTER THREE

THE BASIC PRESUPPOSITIONS OF THE DHARMAŚĀSTRA AND THEIR RELATION TO HINDU SOCIETY

'LAW' (A SACRED NORM) AND LAW (A LEGAL RULE)

All śāstric writers accepted certain presuppositions, which could not be doubted: if they were not accepted the system of thought would collapse. If we were sure that these no longer operated in modern Indian society we should say the śāstra was dead [1]. It is the permanence of these hypotheses which gives the śāstra, in spite of many outgrown rules, its significance for Indology. It may be useful to summarise, if rather inadequately, what the śāstrīs attempted to do, leaving aside the question of the relationship between our śāstra and the arthaśāstra, of which śāstric works take, characteristically, a minimal notice.

Assuming that every individual seeks parama-śreyasa, final beatitude, expressed in whatever language is appropriate to the school of philosophy or sect of religion, the 'ultimate state' whatever its technical name, the śāstra asserts that society, alert for defence and offence, exists not for its own sake (there is none) but in order that this state may be achieved by each inhabitant. To some it presents itself as an alternative: the individual may take the way of the Bhagavadgītā and Manu, and abandon all desire, even desire for transcendental ends; or he may choose to attain supernatural or supersensory ends (as indeed he may aim to achieve worldly ends)—in the first case no effort should be spent which is directed to desire (kāma), one should not perform injunctions which are, in fact, directed to him who has desires, let it be for heaven or for some other end; this is the higher, better path [2]. But in the second case there is available to him, if properly qualified to perform various injunctions, requirements laid down in the Veda and the smṛtis, so that he may achieve more transient ends. Both paths (corresponding to different temperaments) are open, and both are recognised and sanctioned in the śāstra. The Bhagavadgītā rightly insists that professors of religion have no right to dissuade individuals from the path of observances, they

[1] M. Galanter, 'The aborted restoration of "indigenous" law in India', C.S.S.H. 14-1 (1972), 53-70.

[2] References at Derrett, RLSI, 68-70.

can at best urge them to raise, as it were, their concept of the gains to be made from performing them [1].

Characteristically, Indian 'righteousness' does not lay down an exclusively valid way, but 'both this and that are true': this does not mean, however, that no order of preference exists in the abstract. It is presupposed that it is 'better' to aim not at heaven or any specifically desired goal, but to practice contentment and seek the extinction of all desires, putting an end to the sensation of 'mineness', detaching the self from sense objects, freeing the self from pain and from dependence. Observances, by concentrating the mind and objectivising evil, have an effect at once purifying and reforming. This leads, it is presumed, to ultimate bliss, relief from the pain of rebirth in the world. It is assumed that human life is hard, and that action (karma) is ultimately responsible for the quality of rebirth which (it is not doubted) the self will suffer unless its residue of unexpiated, un-counteracted evil karma is spent. This overarching theory is still widely accepted in India and 'further India', whether in the form of superstitious traditional practices such as worship of deities through 'services' performed to images, or in the form of conscious adherence to the so-called 'spiritual' practices of schools or sects, and becoming devotees of a particular teacher. The need for this attitude of dependence on another, especially one who embodies or is thought to embody holiness, or upon ideas or practices, to release the individuals from the trammels of daily life, with a view to a release from birth altogether or at least from a less comfortable rebirth is manifested ubiquitously. There can be little doubt but that this has a function in reconciling Hindus (and, with the lawyers, we may include Jainas, Sikhs, and Buddhists in this name) to the restricted expectations from daily life (quite irrespective of the 'freedoms' nominally enshrined in the Constitution) which the delicately balanced components of life in a caste society impose on all families, a balance (which is a limitation) notably missing from Indian society outside India. Meanwhile the religious charlatans and half-charlatans of today are not less highly respected for their suspected falsity, since the commodity they purvey, the means to make a religious self-prostration, has always been valued irrespective of the quality of the person who mediates this end. In this attitude the śāstris of the pre-British and early British period were at one with modern addicts to religiosity.

The way to achieve good karma and to avoid evil must be taught by teachers. These have to be trained. The śāstra assimilated two roads to achieving merit, avoiding the clash between the two paths of karma (action, sacrificial endeav-

---

[1] Bhagavadgītā III.26.

our) and yoga (devotion, asceticism) which reason could hardly avoid. It grew out of the need to train practitioners in domestic and public sacrifices, for the dharma-sūtras were part of Vedic kalpa-sūtras and the presupposition that innumerable individuals would wish to gain merit by observances was never questioned. For those suitably qualified in past observances to leave the path of observance and take to sannyāsa, entering the path of non-attachment, was natural [1]. Such men had that rare quality, objectivity. Obviously the path of asceticism was an alternative and was chosen by men (and in ancient times by women also) who wanted to avoid responsibility, the inconveniences of hard family life (with its arranged marriages), and boredom. The śāstra has absorbed this obviously accepted way of life by attempting to impose upon it conditions, e.g. that one might leave the path of observances gradually, having performed obligations incumbent on all men. Similarly from the śāstric viewpoint a man might remarry only if his living wife were incompetent in matters of 'dharma and progeny'; but with time the customary right of having more than one wife concurrently pushed the śāstrically imposed conditions into the background. In these respects and in others the śāstra became laxer as time passed. Vyavahāra, indeed, could not be relaxed: penalties would not become less severe as time went on. But the long and perhaps inevitable process of demanding less dispiriting penances from offenders and less unpractical observances from seekers for instant bliss began to operate even before Manu was compiled, and persisted (to some modern critics' disgust) until the end of śāstric composition. The śāstris became satisfied that such progressive relaxation was consistent with the flexibility of a now culturally confident, coherent Hindu society; and unless we accept this point of view it is hard to retain respect for their methods.

Subject to these reservations, the majority of producers and consumers, directors and protectors of the producing elements of society, will enter into the householder stage and perform the obligations cast upon men by nature. It follows that all the panoply of social life can be traced out, regulated, explained as if Hindu ways were the only natural ones, stemming from the Creator (however 'he', or 'it' is visualised), and a tidy, well ordered life, with every action capable of discussion and description can be set out in an easy memorable succession. The task can be fathered on fictitious elders of society, the great-grandfathers, as it were, of the people, ancient sages speaking through the mouths of śāstrīs. The actual authors of the smṛtis, or 'remembered tradition', remain anonymous. Jurists learnt the smṛtis by heart and were able to trace back many customary practices directly or indirectly to the

[1] Lingat, Classical Law (see biblio.), 50-1.

words of the sages who, supposedly, heard the truth about duty from the Self-existent One.

The basic presupposition was that all forms of life (even parasitic communities) were emanations from the creative force, and all had their place in the duty-orientated super-society. Each individual's dharma could be predicated for any situation. The śāstra thus set out to teach the dharmas of the varṇas and mixed varṇas and of the āśramas. If we have as example the king, the norms applicable to him were those of the Kṣatriya and the householder. Part of the dharma of kings was to protect the people, to suppress the bad and to foster the good. In the course of the last duty he would give justice, personally, or through deputies or customary tribunals in whose jurisdiction he acquiesced. The politics of government, the apparatus of choice, and installation of the ruler formed eventually a minor part of the śāstra [1]. Here we are concerned only with portions of the śāstra which would come within the king's purview in the execution of his duties.

The accurate running of dharmic rules in society, whether in the ācāra or the vyavahāra chapters, conduced to the stability of the state, and therefore the working of the śāstra in and through the disposal of litigation would be promoted by a perpetual motion. It was in the king's interest to promote justice, with all the flexibility, common sense, and subject to those, integrity that the śāstra demanded. The śāstris' search for the ultimate bliss of the individual citizen would be facilitated by the stability of the kingdom. Its administration thus gradually came, though somewhat timidly, within the scope of our śāstra, though it really belonged to the arthaśāstra.

What actually occurred is well demonstrated by inscriptions, supplementing the position suggested by the śāstra. The king laid down what rules would be observed in his own court [2]. He sanctioned customs [3], and, on the petition of notables, set up new town customs, sometimes on the model of ancient ones, just as he set up markets and so market towns [4]. There were evidently model charters of customs for newly founded settlements [5]. The king appointed administrators (paying them, unfortunately, by the easiest method,

[1] H. Losch, Rājadharma (Bonn, 1959).

[2] Derrett, RLSI, 148-56.

[3] Ibid., 162-3.

[4] Derrett, The Hoysaḷas (Madras, 1957), 187. Miscellaneous regulations of interest appear at Epigraphia Carnatica III Ml. 114 (A.D. 1331); ibid. IV Nag. 39 (A.D. 1271); ibid., IX Bang. 114-115 (? c. 1262); also A.R. No. 277 of 1913 (Annual Report of Epigraphy, Madras, 1914, 92, § 18).

[5] So A.R. (= Annual Report (sc. of Epigraphy)) No. 429 of 1918 and No. 538 of 1918 (the remarks at (Govt. of Madras: Home (Education) Dept.) Annual Report on Epigraphy for the Year Ending 31st March 1919, pp. 37, 45 are quite inadequate).

namely out of the revenues of their area). He could not avoid, from time to time, encroaching on areas for which rules were prescribed in the śāstra, seeing how much of the practical working of life had come within its scope. Fortunately the śāstra itself recognised that the rules of its vyavahāra portion were derived from custom ultimately and did not have, in their detail, a superstitious significance [1]. But any part of the śāstra which dealt with sacraments (saṃskāras), with necessary prayers and charities, with the acquisition of merit by observances or austerities, must remain, in the typical śāstric view, beyond his capacity [2]. The king's regulations must be obeyed, as a matter of conscience [3], but they were valid only so far as they did not encroach upon the scheme of dharma, not only because it was dharma that upheld the king, so that an undharmic king might have to face a revolution [4], but also because the king was the servant of dharma, not its master. While Law, the sacred norm, was an overarching theoretical system directed towards the achievement of dharma by the individual, law, with a minuscule, was the legal rule which happened to run from time to time in the court. The latter would be dharmic in so far as it conformed to the śāstric precept, if this could be found. To this end the śāstris made very infrequent reference to custom since, in their view, it was the practice of the good alone which could form a source of law, and that too only where all other sources were silent. The śāstrī who acted as assessor would advise what the śāstra required, and the judge would decide as policy and good government prompted: the two might coincide, but they often would not.

No rule of law was necessarily drawn from a śāstric text, however apposite. An inapposite text might provide an analogy, and a rule of the mīmāṃsā, originally devised for ritual needs [5], might show how a text, apparently relevant, need not settle the matter, while another, apparently less relevant, should sway the judge's mind.

The moral qualities of the nation, the ultimate virtues, must be subserved in any event. These were truth, abstention from injuring, freedom from anger, humanity, self-control, uprightness, abstention from theft, ritual purity, restraint of the appetites, generosity, compassion, discrimination, forbearance, absence of envy, abstention from violence, patience, freedom

---

[1] The Bhaviṣya-purāṇa in a celebrated five-fold distinction: Kane, HD, III, 840-1.

[2] Derrett, RLSI, 167, citing Devaṇṇa-bhaṭṭa (13th cent.).

[3] Manu VII.13, discussed at Derrett, JAOS, 84/4 (1964), 392-5; Kane: HD, I², 569-70.

[4] Note the allegation contained in the imaginary conversation at Kauṭilya, Arthaśāstra I.10.2-4, adopted into dharmaśāstra by Bhāruci and Medhātithi (Derrett, ZDMG, 115/1, 1965, 145).

[5] Kane, HD, V, chh. 28-30.

from meanness, regard for the interests of others [1]. The judicial officer should see how these could be met in the individual case, for it is evident that litigation would have been avoided if these had been observed. The śāstrī was a referee, and would naturally defer to a scholar of greater wisdom and experience, still more to a committee of scholars, a pariṣad, to which a tricky or highly disputed problem would be referred. Specialists in dharma were appointed to villages and towns, as is known [2], and a single jurist could be called pariṣad [3], perhaps honorifically and in any case in conformity with smṛti provisions. Numerous jurist-authors were themselves appointed as dharmic advisers (the word dharmādhikārī does not necessarily imply Chief Justice as is so often assumed) [4]. That śāstric texts in abundance were consulted in contexts where law, society, and religion overlapped is proved by other inscriptions [5]. Still others mention the existence, here and there throughout the countryside of men with a reputation for specialist knowledge in the dharmaśāstra along with other śāstras, so as to amount to one-man universities of polymathic versatility [6].

In the early British period traditional methods were frequently employed, both in the course of litigation and in preparation for it or an attempt to avoid it [7]. In 1864 reference to living professors of the śāstra was terminated

---

[1] Texts collected by Derrett at Critique, app. to ch. 2.

[2] Epigraphia Indica 37 (1968), No. 50 (iii), p. 287, ll. 16-19 (A.D. 1054).

[3] E.g. Vācaspati-miśra (15th cent.).

[4] E.g. Caṇḍeśvara (14th cent.). The qualifications of the dharmādhikārī (judge) as distinguished from the smārta (expert in dharma) are set out nicely in Mānasollāsa I.ii.94-5 (Shama Sastry) cf. I, 1255. See also D.C. Sircar, 'Dharmādhikaraṇa and dharmādhikārin', Purāṇa 6/2 (1964), 445-50.

[5] Annual Report of South Indian Epigraphy 1936-7, No. 135, pp. 91ff., sec. 79 (Derrett, RLSI, 168); A. R. No. 558 of 1904 (= South Indian Inscriptions XVII, 1964, No. 603); A. R. No. 479 of 1908; A. R. No. 189 of 1925 (Derrett, in Prof. K. A. Nilakanta Sastri 80th Birthday Felicitation Volume, Madras, 1971, 32-55). See also V. Raghavan, 'The Vaiśyavaṃśasudhākara', Vol. Pres. to Sir Denison Ross (Bombay, 1939), 234-40 (Kane, HD, III, 252 n.). Surviving documents prove the currency of śāstric jargon and ideas: Kane, ibid., 381. Inscriptional evidence of litigation is similarly consistent: e.g. Bombay-Karṇāṭak Inscriptions IV (1965), No. 232 (A.D. 1412); No. 391 (A.D. 1538). On brahmins as law-teachers see H. Hosten on Fr. A. Monserrate, S.J., (A.D. 1579), at JASB, NS, 18 (1922), 349-69.

[6] Epigraphia Carnatica VII Sk. 105 (A.D. 1193); Epigraphia Indica V, 221-2 (A. Lorenzen at ABORI, 52, 1971, 97-139 at 104-5, 126-7). Ibid. XV, No. 24 (348ff.) (A.D. 1098) (Someśvarabhaṭṭa, dharmaśāstrī, founds a school for the study of the Prābhākara (!) system of Pūrvamīmāṃsā at Lokkiguṇḍi/Gadag).

[7] Kane, HD, III, 684 n. 1294 (on Rāmśāstrī, the Peshwa's dharmādhikārī). S. Sen and U. Mishra, Sanskrit Documents (Allahabad, 1951); Subhadra Jha, ed., Dharmaśāstrīya vyavasthāsaṃgraha (Allahabad, 1957). V. N. Mandlik, Vyavahāra Mayūkha (Bombay 1880), 475-7.

by statute, and recurred only when judges thought expert testimony ought to be called to settle something which the known books (as too often) left vague. This could be regretted, and the Privy Council in London decided questions of Hindu law with the aid of translations of Sanskrit books, making what sense they could of them, and being moved, silently, by the tendency of Indian case-law to reflect the preferences of the public. At the very commencement of the British period the practice must have reproduced what previous rulers used to do. Two reports were called for: from the revenue department as to what the practice was, and what would be the effects of a particular solution; and from the śāstrī or śāstrīs as to what the śāstra prescribed. The very dissimilar reports would then be examined in an effort to see which would be the best solution [1].

The British and post-British methods, though they dispensed with recourse to living repositories of learning after 1864, were ultimately not altogether dissimilar from the previous.

The apparent dissimilarity, worth emphasis, lies in the fact that foreign rulers never referred to Hindu ethical principles and placed far too much weight on the śāstric texts available to them, unaware that they were not law books in the Western sense [2], and tended to confine books to regional schools (on the 'reception' theory adverted to above), a notion unknown to śāstric theory [3]. Thus they at one and the same time raised the practical significance of the śāstra, and hampered its free and natural operation. On the other hand, insensibly and gradually, certain adjustments in the law took place in response to the evident needs of the public. But in formal terms the ancient texts themselves were as much the basic authorities in 1945 as they had been in 1745 or 1645. Indian judges brought up in the Anglo-Indian system, and esteemed by their superiors to be fit for a judgeship, made as hesitant and infrequent reference to Indian conditions and Indian preferences as their foreign rulers: since India was a large unstable amalgam of thousands of castes, it is understandable that this should be so. Indian judges were aware, during the British period, that the śāstra did not correspond with customs contemporary with themselves, but, along with their British colleagues, they totally rejected the notion of Nelson that non-Brahminical communities should be presumed not to be governed by the śāstra,

[1] Records referred to by Derrett at C.S.S.H. 4/1 (1961), 52.

[2] L. Rocher, 'De historische grondslagen van het oud-Indische recht', Indonesië 10 (1957), 472-95.

[3] L. Rocher, 'Schools of Hindu Law', India Maior (Jan Gonda Fel. Vol.) (Leiden, 1972), 167-76.

of which they had no knowledge [1]. For, until 1857, were not the most ignorant peasants of England governed, in matters of matrimony and testamentary succession, by the Canon law works, all of which were in Latin (and guides to them in English were few and in any case unavailable to illiterates), and wherever Common law intervened to provide the rule of decision, were not the secondary writings as obscure to the populace as the original authorities, many of which were in a variety of French which would be unintelligible even in France? Manifestly, courts were not confined in their search for legal sources to materials within the knowledge of the public! We know that in medieval India the unlearned public would from time to time insist upon their śāstrīs' expounding crucial stanzas in the regional language [2]; during the British period large areas of Indian law, including the personal laws in their Anglo-Indian guise, were made available to the literate but lay reader in vernacular works of various degrees of adequacy; but the overall decline in contact between those who reported on the academic position and the public for whose benefit it was reported reflected the defensive position which Nelson and his few supporters inspired: the law, purporting to be based on the wisdom of ancient sages, and tempered through the wisdom of British or English-trained Indian 'sages', did not emerge from the consciousness of the people, and did not purport to move in response to the demands of most of them, or to acknowledge, let alone respond to, the needs of the lower, that is to say, majority classes of the Hindu public.

In this curious doubly élitist approach the body of pleaders and advocates played no heroic part. Their earnings depended on their happy relationship with the judiciary. Many studied the śāstra as a hobby, but there were no movements towards bringing back the law into touch with the people. It might have been otherwise if the śāstra had contained a tradition of lay participation. There were no professional advocates in ancient India [3]. The insertion of provisions relating to such in the Śukra-nītisāra are amongst those proving its modernity. It is usually supposed that the absence of advocates assisted the discovery of the truth, as in modern panchayat courts [4]; but this, while it proves how judicial decisions could add nothing to law and were unworthy of study in their own right (cases never made law), also

1 Derrett, RLSI, 230 n., 292 n.; Lingat, Classical Law, 138-9, 141.

2 S.I.I. XVII, No. 603, cited at p. 23, n. 5.

3 L. Rocher, '"Lawyers" in classical Hindu Law', Law and Society Review 3/2 (1968-9), 383-402. On the profession today the same volume contains invaluable articles, see also Charles Morrison, 'Munshis and their Masters', J. Asian Studies 31/2 (1972), 309-28; the same 'Kinship in professional relations', C.S.S.H. 14/1 (1972) 100-125.

4 Govt. of India. Ministry of Law. Report of the Study Team on Nyaya Panchayats (April 1962) (New Delhi, 1962).

fits a judicial system in which all the advantage lies with the court's ascertainment of the true factors and the true facts in the litigation; whereas the ascertainment of the norm, the ideal law, is left to the specialist, the śāstrī in this case, whose prescription in no sense emerged from the actual facts of the case, unless he was corrupted by one or both parties. Advocacy in modern India has not assisted the development of juridical studies, but it has provided a large body of men and women in touch with real-life situations, impatient of any lack of realism in the decisions of the courts which they may themselves constitute if they accept judgeships, and whose performance they constantly watch, alert, from habit, for any sign of inconsistency or incompetence. This naturally leads us to consider the weaknesses of the traditional system.

CHAPTER FOUR

INTELLECTUAL WEAKNESSES IN THE DHARMAŚĀSTRA AND ITS DRAWBACKS

ITS CONTRIBUTION TO INDOLOGY AND THE WORLD'S EXPERIENCE

If we think of the śāstra as a body of literature, a continuity of living tradition (moving steadily nearer to obsolescence), it was a great weakness that it did not more prominently, and more frequently define its own function, and distinguish it from that of the judge. It was also a weakness to assume, from the public's preference for the myth that all norms emanated from a superhuman source, that innovation was decay, and that change must be, not merely for the worse, but an infringement of the natural order of things. From the static and statuesque appearance of the śāstra, its sources and style alike suggesting that Law is immutable (sanātana) whatever the motion of actual practices, it has been concluded in modern times that smṛti even provided a model, deplorable but powerful, for other areas of literature [1], whose general want (if we exclude Pāṇini) of major original inspiration and lack of flexibility is so notable. On the contrary a static society, moving, if at all, without admitting change, naturally lacks desire for native original inspiration, and India has depended on foreign stimulus, directly or indirectly, for producing some of her most exacting and praiseworthy achievements. The weakness of the śāstra reflected the weakness of such a society, when faced with the massive stimuli of the mid-nineteenth to mid-twentieth century.

All writers who operated in law (but not all historians) [2] became obsessed with the notion that the śāstra was, at least in some of its ācāra and all of its vyavahāra portions, a potential code of law, and that if it did not resemble the work of Justinian's team under Tribonian the fault was not of those that asked questions Tribonian sought to answer, but of the śāstris who compiled the Hindu literature! From the publication of Jagannātha's Vivādabhaṅgārṇava, typically referred to as Colebrooke's Digest (though Colebrooke merely translated it), a work which disappointed the European judges for

---

1 S. N. Dasgupta, History of Sanskrit Literature, I² (Calcutta, 1962), xxiii.

2 Govind Das, Introduction to the Vyavahāra-Bālambhaṭṭī (Chowkhambā Skt. Ser., Benares, 1914).

whose use it was written [1], the habit began of construing texts as evidence of what Hindus did and enforced as law in pre-British times. This simple, but erroneous, equation suited the curiosity of comparative lawyers and Sanskritists, who began to delve into the texts and to expound the results as 'ancient Indian law'. [2] Mazzarella, Cunha Gonçalves, and more recently Ruben, proceeded on this hypothesis in various ways. For Indians minded as was Jayaswal it was a matter of pride that the ancient civilization had produced a monument of learning equal to that produced by the admired Romans. Had the nature and extent of Jewish law been known, a different conclusion might have been arrived at. This mode of thought led to twin ends, each deplorable. James Mill, Mountstuart Elphinstone, Sir Henry Maine, and others decried the Hindu law as lacking in completeness, objectivity, and realism [3]. Their opponents, P. N. Sen, N. C. Sen-Gupta, Kane, Rangaswami Aiyangar, Varadachariar and others depicted the śāstra as authentic evidence of what was, with the utmost efficiency and insight, administered in most if not all pre-British tribunals.

Either judgment was false. Juridical development was more sophisticated than the former suggests; yet the prestige and elaboration of the śāstra stood as a veritable obstacle to judicial expertise, and to any legislative change which could supplement or correct it. Kane's work is the best specimen of its kind. It defends India against Western scepticism, but at the same time effectually tended to secure India against a real, conscious, intellectually articulate continuity with her own past by bewailing her seemingly amateurish and muddle-headed 'departures' from the śāstra. The whole story of the abrogation of traditional norms, which patriots hardly knew whether to deplore or to laud, to condemn as infractions of Hinduism, or to praise as evidence of India's membership of a cosmopolitan, secular world, is a story

---

[1] Note Colebrooke's preface to his translation of it, and the disparaging remarks referring to it in F. W. Macnaghten's Considerations on the Hindoo Law (Serampore, 1824).

[2] European interest is exemplified in A. F. Stenzler, 'Die Indischen Gottesurtheile', ZDMG 9 (1885), 661-82; Cândido de Figueiredo, A Penalidade na Índia segundo o Código de Manú (Lisbon, 1892); V. Manzini, 'La procedura ordalica ...', Atti del Reale Ist. Veneto di Sc., Lett., ed Arti, 63/2 (1903-4), 333-58; V. Rocca, I giudizi di Dio (Livorno, 1904); D. Makrydimas, La royauté hindoue d'après des codes brahmaniques (Trieste, 1923). The presence in this short list of three works on ordeals is due to European recognition that it was an institution which connected India, Judaism, and the West.

[3] Sir Henry Maine said (31 Mar. 1866), 'To an English lawyer all Hindú law appears like law in the gaseous, or at most fluid, condition ... It does seem to me, so long as this theory of a Kali Yuga is maintained, it is quite impossible to come to a positive conclusion on any part of the Hindu law that had not been sanctioned by constant usage or decided expressly by judicial authority'. Gazette of India, Supplement, 1866, p. 212.

which would be too long to tell in this chapter, but must be alluded to again below.

In reality the value of the śāstra could have been more highly estimated on both wings of the controversy. Collectively, over more than twentyfive centuries, śāstrīs had worked out a system of thought containing a body of detailed rules, tackling every facet of life. In their view the question of the *suitability* of rules of law, e.g. whether a child over five might be adopted, could hardly be broached, since it had been worked out finally over centuries by learned Brahmins whose lives bore out all the moral requirements set out above. This certified the fitness of the rule. Unless such Brahmins had adopted a practice, it could never find its place in the śāstra, and could be taken seriously then only if a text, already of some age, had crystallized it. This weakness emerged clearly when the British asked śāstrīs their opinion on the legality of abolishing the slave-trade, or even slavery itself. To deviate from an established rule, however, would be to forfeit membership of the caste. A conservative, relatively immobile society could not face rebellion, which could be seen only as the work of evil forces. Recalcitrant, factious elements must be put down by the king (Nārada X.5). If the king himself (in the person of the East India Company or the British Crown) were to disown or manipulate the śāstra, the support of the system was cut at the root.

The position is illustrated by the extremely trying example of the marriage of a boy with his maternal uncle's daughter. The solution to the problem proves that, at its furthest stretch, the śāstra barely managed to admit a notorious custom which had been in use for a millennium at the least. The reason for the custom was economic. No question of the couple's personal preference arose. With enormous ingenuity the esoteric principles of sapiṇḍaship were flexed to accommodate the custom subject to certain conditions, which by no means covered the majority of cases. Sapiṇḍaship is the close blood relationship which operates in the fields of pollution at death, community in offerings to a deceased relative, and the prohibited degrees for marriage. Modern critics would find some rationalistic grounds for the archaic principles but what interests us is the need felt by jurists, from areas where such a custom as we have described was in use, to try to bring the custom within the general rules. The need arose not out of compassion, but the fact that learned Brahmins had long followed this custom. Provided these did not intermarry with 'orthodox' Brahmins, each practice could be accepted as sanctioned by occult forces which in either case were conservative and constituted no threat to the overarching concept of law and morality. We may fruitfully contrast, to India's disadvantage, the two great schools of Pharisaism amongst the Jews roughly contemporary with the conflict we have mentioned as acutely troublesome to the śāstrīs. The Hillelites differed on very many points from the Shammaïtes, including many which invaded the routine of the household: yet the Mishnah tells us [1] that there was intermarriage between the two sub-schools, so that each accepted the other as intellectually sound, even though their practices were often irreconcilable. This degree of tolerance began to arrive in British and post-British India slowly, and as a distinctly modern departure, inconsistent with traditional ways.

Yet what was a weakness, from a modern viewpoint, also demonstrated a discovery which is indeed India's own. Coexistence, balance between castes and sub-castes, tolerance of the persistence of deviations (even very bizarre ways of life): this was characteristic of India. It was a small price to pay for peace in a vast country with few natural frontiers, subject to frequent invasions, and constant minor migrations. But the special isolation which this presupposed between each unit of society ceased to be valid when vast new expectations and ambitions were created, out of European penetration and rule, by India's admirable facility for emulation. The scorn of Indian practices and beliefs all to frankly revealed by Europeans touched deeply the Indian concern for prestige. Many an oddity of socio-religious life rapidly disappeared, religious suicides at Prayāga and elsewhere, *satī* (abolished in 1829), female infanticide, hook-swinging, and self-mortification by professional sureties of high caste: these faded from the scene as did many bizarre elements in religious art, as a response to European criticism. Hindu revival movements, defensively incorporating Christian notions under the guise of a return to proto-Hindu purity, moved pari passu with a new attitude to society and to mobility within it.

There is a difference between suppressing as a matter of royal regulation something that had previously been allowed (as the dedication of girls to be devadāsīs was prohibited in Bombay and Madras, and cow-slaughter was prohibited in many North Indian States after Independence), and accepting something which denied the validity of the system itself. It was bad enough to think of mlecchas as rulers; how could one accept as a marriage (as distinct from concubinage) a union between a Śūdra male and a twice-born female, or a Brahmin male with a widow or divorcee? The śāstra could, as long as it was interpreted with the aid of Kumārila-bhaṭṭa (a scholar in the mīmāṃsā over a millenium ago), never find room for positive innovations stemming from others than Brahmins learned in the whole of the Veda. The concept of loka-vidviṣṭa-garhana, whereby practices which were enshrined in the

[1] Mishnah, Eduyot IV. 8 (H. Danby, The Mishnah, Oxford, 1933, 429-30).

śāstra might nevertheless be abandoned if they were abhorred by the public [1], would not serve to authorise the introduction of *new* practices.

The fault of a highly intellectual, comprehensive system of thought, especially one devised by generations of pedants inclined to encyclopedism, as the Brahmins were, is that it stultifies growth, defies and discourages new ideas, and provides a powerful systematic hindrance to innovation. The position is *not* improved if the theories are based on centuries of essential empirical research, if the empiricism of our own day truly invalidates it. The theory that new munis are called for, a new śāstra, taken seriously by so eminent a thinker as S. Radhakrishnan [2], President (then) of India, was wishful thinking with no foundation in the śāstra itself. The need to enable Hindus to marry non-Hindus had, indeed, been solved by the Special Marriage Act [3]; statute provided, too, for the needs of a sect or group of Hindus wishing to marry without traditional Hindu ceremonial [4]. The coherence of the śāstra would not be threatened by such innovations. When it became obvious that radical reforms were called for, when piecemeal tinkering which merely amended a few rules [5] gave way to an intellectual scheme for total revision in the field of the family law, opposition to all reform exploited the incompatibility of the propositions argued for with the śāstric component of Hinduness [6]; while some sections of the parties supporting reform tried to show (much less convincingly) that some of the reforms were anticipated in known or less known texts, if properly interpreted [7]. In 1955-6 the reformers' scheme came to partial fruition.

The leading principles were to equate, so far as might be, the rights of females with those of males, and to remove the rules which created distinctions between varṇas. They were not applied thoroughly, but they were applied significantly. Amongst the more remarkable changes effected in 1955-6

---

1 References at Derrett, RLSI, 89-90.

2 Foreword to P.H. Valavalkar's Hindu Social Institutions (Bombay, 1939); Foreword to Kane, HD, V (see Derrett, RLSI, 29 n. 1). See also the activities of the Dharma-nirṇaya-maṇḍala of Wai and Lonavla: Kane, HD, V, 1705.

3 Act 43 of 1954, repealing and replacing Act 3 of 1872.

4 Hindu Marriage (Madras Amendment) Act, 21 of 1967.

5 Well summarised in Kane, HD, III, 820-4.

6 Derrett, cited p. 5, n. 4. See also T. K. Tope and H. S. Ursekar, Why Hindu Code? (Lonavla, 1953) also P. B. Gajendragndkar, 'The Hindu Code Bill' (1951) in V. D. Mahajan (cit. sup.) at pp. 240-98 (pro-codification). Why Hindu Code is Detestable[3] (Calcutta, Shastra Dharma Prachar Sabha, N. D. (1956)). V. V. Deshpande, Dharmaśāstra and the Proposed Hindu Code (Benares, 1943). Narendranath Set, Third Hindu Code (Calcutta, 1944). See also various articles in the Silver Jubilee Number of the Madras Law Journal (1941).

7 B. N. Chobe, Principles of Dharmashastr (Hyderabad, N.D. (1949 ?)).

were these: polygamous marriages became illegal and punishable, and existing polygamous unions could be dissolved on the ground that another wife of the respondent still lived; divorce was introduced; the law of nullity was expanded and clarified; females could be adopted, and women could adopt in their own right; the right of an adopted son to acquire interests in the property that belonged to the family of his adoptive father (deceased) was greatly reduced; the special rights of the illegitimate son of a Śūdra were abolished so far as succession was concerned; the law of succession was modified to allow remoter relations to inherit, but the propositus was allowed much greater freedom of testation and female heirs were allowed to hold property absolutely where previously they had taken a limited estate; further all females holding limited estates when the Hindu Succession Act came into force were advantaged by having their estate converted into an absolute estate forthwith. There were a great many more adjustments which, substantial in appearance, would affect the public less drastically in practice: such was the reduction in the number of degrees of sapiṇḍaship as a bar to marriage; and such, as the experience of India since 1956 reveals, was the grant of an equal share in her father's property to a daughter. whether married or unmarried (!), in competition with her own brother [1]. Such new rights were not employed, on the whole, so as to defeat the customary behaviour of families in these important contexts of marriage and inheritance.

The superimposition of this brief 'Code' onto a vast and intricate system such as the Anglo-Hindu law (which naturally continues to exist in Pakistan, Bangladesh, Burma, Malaysia and Singapore), abolishing so much of the previous law as was incompatible with its provisions, and no more, naturally raised major questions of interpretation. With many varieties of viewpoint in between them two poles of opinion emerged. The first is based upon cultural continuity, supposing that the sediment of millennia of legal development has received a new layer, namely the 'Hindu Code', and that where this is unclear the practice and principles of former periods must be looked to sympathetically. Many decisions of the courts, especially in the realm of adoption, and to some degree in that of marriage and divorce, take this view. The Hindu law, in its traditional guise, is occasionally consulted even in contexts removed from the topics governed by the personal law [2]. Cultural continuity is also supported by the Supreme Court's handling of the right

[1] Hindu Succession Act, 30 of 1956, secs. 8, 10, and Schedule.

[2] State of Bombay v. Chamarbaugwala (1957) 59 Bombay Law Reporter 945; Gherulal v. Mahadeodas (1959) 22 Supreme Court Journal 878; Giri v. Suri Dora AIR 1959 S.C. 1318; Qureshi v. State of Bihar AIR 1958 S.C. 731; Kunhikannan v. State of Kerala 1958 Kerala Law Times 19 at p. 23.

of a religious head to excommunicate an offender for breaches of the religious discipline of the community [1]; and by the delicate manner in which the conflict between the need for State control of public places of worship. and the need of the community to secure that worship be conducted in an orthodox manner, is handled by that supreme tribunal [2].

There is an opposite pole. Many universities teach all the personal laws concurrently as Family Law. This encourages a cosmopolitan and up-to-date outlook, which is the only common denominator of approaches to the various personal laws. A forward-looking interpretation of the 'Hindu Code' sides with the New India. This sees the legislation as abrogating the spirit and the style of the Anglo-Hindu law, and substituting for it new institutions which cannot, for their own interpretation, take any light from previous principles or practices. Thus Hindu marriage, in this view, is not a new variety of traditional Hindu marriage, but a new institution owing little to the past, and sufficient to the West to make it altogether possible to construe the Hindu Marriage Act with the aid of English law [3]. The New-India interpretation finds numerous instances in recent Indian legal history to support it. The Constitution guarantees only those freedoms which public policy upheld, and many Hindu principles were sacrificed when the Constitution was framed [4]. It was discovered that several customs and traditional usages familiar to Hinduism were abrogated by the Fundamental Rights [5]. Some ancient Hindu usages have failed to stand the test of judicial scrutiny, and have passed from the realm of law into that of social practice [6]. The extraordinary efforts made to give privileges to the pariahs and other Backward Classes, known as 'protective discrimination', are politically, and no doubt economically desirable [7], but hostile to the traditional Hindu outlook, which saw in the poverty and backwardness of those classes a natural sequel to their crimes in previous lives. To quote only a remarkable instance of the want of regard for Hindu sentiment, the legislation authorising

---

1 Sardar Syedna v. State of Bombay AIR 1962 S.C. 853. Derrett, RLSI, 473-7. U.C. Sarkar, Law Review (Punjab) 19/1 (1967), 16-17.

2 E. R. J. Swami v. State of Tamil Nad AIR 1972 S.C. 1586.

3 B. N. Sampath, review article in J.I.L.I. 14/3 (1972), 443-58. For a specimen of such decision making see Madhukar v. Saral (1971) 74 Bombay Law Reporter 496.

4 Constitution, Artt. 25, 26 ('subject to public order, morality and health ...'); cf. Art. 17.

5 Derrett, Critique, 405 and n. 8.

6 I. N. Sampathkumar v. I. N. S. Andalamma AIR 1969 A.P. 303 (Full Bench).

7 Constitution, Artt. 15 (4), 16 (4). M. Galanter, at Rutgers Law Review 16/1 (1961), 42-74; J.I.L.I. 3/2 (1961), 205-34; Asian Survey 3/11 (1963), 544-59; I.Y.B.I.A. 1965, 257-80; J. Asian & African Stud. 2/1-2 (1967), 91-124; in M. Singer and B. S. Cohn, edd., Structure and Change in Indian Society (Chicago, 1968), 299-336; Philosophy E. & W. 21/4 (1971), 467-87.

abortion and sterilisation, and particularly the former, cuts across the Hindu concept of procreation and defies the Hindu notion that 'killing of an embryo' is a great sin. It is very difficult to see how there could be a useful compromise between the opposite points of view, since a legal decision can hardly be both traditional and revolutionary, progressive and conservative.

After the 'Hindu Code' nothing stood in the way of the formulation of a Civil Code for all Indians but the timidity of the government, the intransigence of Muslims, and the want of technical skill. Freedom also has a negative side. The intellectual vacuum left by the uncertainty described above was matched by the vacuum left by the destruction of the old comprehensive system of law as a unit. What remained in the law of the Joint Family was emasculated as it was cut off from the parent body of the śāstra in any case. No coherent principles of all-India ethics and rightness existed with the aid of which a modern cosmopolitan substitute for the personal laws could be construed. There was no all-India platform from which to survey the ruins of Anglo-Hindu law, to appraise what has been achieved by the Hindu Code, and to recommend its extension, development, or further reform. The learned annual surveys produced by the Indian Law Institute (New Delhi) are most informative, but not least in their proof that no directing mind surveys what happens and what might yet happen.

Unlike many countries with highly reformed traditional laws (e.g. Japan, Turkey, Iran), India does indeed work her legal system, for it serves many psychological needs and is a genuine feature of her daily existence; but she is still searching for a substitute for her śāstra. It will be through a myriad of judicial decisions that she will recreate faith in the continuity of Indian tradition, even in the legal field, where reforms based ultimately on cosmopolitan experience (e.g. adoption, or divorce) appear, at first sight, to be fatal to continuity. To many minds this may seem plausible, since it has been of the essence of Hinduness to seem to change, but to remain substantially the same.

The śāstra has not utterly deserted its public, merely because the court-law has changed. Ancient patterns of behaviour are still with us. The arranged marriage, with all its anomalous results, shows no signs of disappearing, and the greater freedom accorded to women in law serves rather to expose the shortcomings of that system than alleviate them. The authority of parents is not noticeably reduced. Superficial westernization does not remove from literature, teaching, and habit ubiquitous evidence of the persistence of traditional mores and standards. The vyavahāra section of the śāstra seldom figures grandly in law contexts; but the public are still very much aware of prāyaścitta, pūjā, śrāddha and tīrtha. Astrologers and genealogists proceed as if the śāstra had not been affected by legislation; conspicuous ceremonies, from the most common, such as upanayana and vivāha, to the most uncommon, such as would come within pratiṣṭhā, and the rarer ceremonials within karma-vipāka, and the still rarer Vedic sacrificial performances, all bring the śāstra into the limelight, indulgently regarded by the young who, as the circle comes round, will find significance in them in old age.

Accepting that the śāstra must live on in the rather insecure world of ethics, as a key to much in the epics, classical, and neo-classical literature [1], it is a matter of concern whether academic study of the śāstra will survive. As in other regions, Indian legal history demands more expertise than other branches of history which are less capable of verification and less subject to control by the context. Legal history cannot be selectively investigated and taught, and there is less room for subjective apprehension and motivation. The urge to present India's indigenous law gloriously, and to compare unfavourably with it whatever Europe has produced, disappeared shortly after India attained Independence. To illuminate dark passages in general history, as to explain many a dark chapter of the substantive law, Indian legal history retains a considerable potential.

The śāstra is richly suited to clarifying the Indian mentality, since what is taught in it, though no longer explaining what (as was supposed) used to happen in Indian law-courts, in reality distils the refined norms approved by a nation that never recognised a competing legal and ethical system. Here jurisprudence and the rules of law, self-consciously developed as far as was required for the limited purposes described above, offered a mirror to all Indian social groups except the pariahs. Thus India's indigenous standards, her expectations from life, and not least what she did not expect from it, are faithfully shown. Her great contribution to world experience was the detailed working out of the coexistence of social units, co-development without mutual penetration. The śāstra's deep devotion to the psychological needs of the individual makes especially good sense when we realise that the individual never counted at all as a legal and social entity: the balance between groups depended upon his submerging himself, in the secular sense, and in order to do this he abstracted himself in the spiritual sense. This achievement, which has no counterpart, can be the more readily investigated now it is understood that law subserved the śāstra—the śāstra was not invented to subserve law. 'Liberty' and 'equality', as ideals, were unknown to the śāstra, which could have found small scope for them in

---

[1] L. Sternbach, Juridical Studies in Ancient Indian Law, 2 vols. (Delhi, 1965-7); also at JAOS, 88/3 (1968), 495-520, and J. Ganganatha Jha Kendriya Sanskrit Vidyapeetha 27/1-2 (1971), 167-260.

daily life. A higher standard is required from any sympathetic inquirer of our own age.

The obstacles to study are the want of Sanskrit (accentuated by translations subtly biassed in favour of a wrong view of what the books aimed to achieve) and the newcomer's reluctance to accept, for purposes of argument, the propositions concerning karma and rebirth which the śāstra takes for granted. It may be that educational opportunities on the one hand, and the discovery that our Western systems too have their unexpressed, and too seldom explored, presuppositions which amount to superstitions (e.g. 'progress', 'productivity'), will link hands with the gradual increase in objectivity in India's own attitudes to her traditions, so as to reassure the comparative student of institutions and law that he has in the śāstra a worthy field of comparison with the medieval West. Like can be compared with like. The overarching scheme of the śāstra will not act as a deterrent when it is seen as inessential to the material itself. A better study of inscriptional evidence and records of customs will reassure the student that the śāstra's handling of its raw ingredients was arrangement, selection, explanation, and exhortation, rather than sophistication.

On the other hand it is essential, if the śāstra is to be used as a branch of Indology, that it should be approached as a whole. No śāstrī was unaware that the arthaśāstra or nītiśāstra existed. No student of vyavahāra was unaware of prāyaścitta. Rules from one chapter should not be taken literally in ignorance that, in an adjacent chapter, something existed to qualify it. Historians do wrong to take a verse from its context and rely on it in vacuo. The science was studied, in its prime, by students who devoted many years to it, and little can be understood by subjectively-directed gleaning here and there.

It will be insufficient to proceed as the British, misled by medieval jurists' tendentious reliance on mīmāṃsā techniques, often did, viz. pretending that the sages spoke with one voice, when there were, in fact, a great many unresolved alternatives. The fact that many possibilities were equally consistent with dharma should be taken seriously and students of any problem, e.g. feudalism, will easily be misled if they extrapolate too soon from our texts a fully-finished and coherent answer to problems arising outside the śāstra. The difficulties of detailed and patient work, comparable perhaps with those of mastering astronomical or algebraical literature, should not be alleged as a reason for giving inadequate answers, or, alternatively ignoring what the śāstra has to offer. In other words cooperative work in called for, and Indian legal history may well emerge as a science in its own right.

BIBLIOGRAPHY

Bibliographical aids

L. Rocher, 'Droit Hindou Ancien', E/6 in J. Gilissen, ed., Introduction Bibliographique à l'Histoire du Droit et à l'Ethnologie Juridique (Bruxelles, 1965).

J. D. M. Derrett, 'The Indian Subcontinent under European Influence', E/8 ibid. (Bruxelles, 1969).

C. H. Alexandrowicz, A Bibliography of Indian Law (Oxford, 1958).

H. C. Jain, Indian Legal Materials (Bombay/Dobbs Ferry, 1970).

See also Lingat (below); Derrett (1968) (below).

J. D. M. Derrett, Dharmaśāstra and Juridical Literature, in J. Gonda, ed., History of Indian Literatures, IV (Wiesbaden, 1973).

The Dharmaśāstra

G. Mazzarella, Etnologia analitica dello antico diritto indiano (Catania, 1913-38) (see Derrett, ZVR, 71/1, 1969, 1-44).

J. C. Ghose, Principles of Hindu Law^{3} (Calcutta, 1917-19).

P. N. Sen, General Principles of Hindu Jurisprudence (Calcutta, 1918).

C. Sankararama Sastri, Fictions in the Development of the Hindu Law Texts (Madras, 1926).

G. C. Sarkar Sastri, Treatise on Hindu Law^{6} (Calcutta, 1927).

G. Jha, Hindu Law in its Sources (Allahabad, 1930-1).

P. V. Kane, History of Dharmaśāstra, 5 vols. in 7 (Poona, 1930- 62); I/1 revised edn. (Poona, 1968).

L. S. Joshi, Dharmakośa, Vyavahāra-kāṇḍa (Wai, 1937-41).

L. da Cunha Gonçalves, Direito hindú e mahometano (Coimbra, 1924).

J. Jolly, Recht und Sitte (Strassburg, 1896), trans., Hindu Law and Custom (Calcutta, 1928).

M. Das, The Hindu Law of Bailment (Khulna, 1946).

K. V. Rangaswami Aiyangar, Some Aspects of the Hindu View of Life according to Dharmaśāstra (Baroda, 1952).

L. Renou and J. Filiozat, L'Inde Classique, I (Paris, 1947), 859-79.

N. C. Sen-Gupta, Evolution of Ancient Indian Law (Calcutta/London, 1953).

P. N. Prabhu, Hindu Social Organization (Bombay, 1954).

J. R. Gharpure, Teachings of Dharmaśāstra (Lucknow, 1956).

S. K. Maitra, Ethics of the Hindus (Calcutta, 1956).

K. R. R. Sastry, Hindu Jurisprudence (Calcutta, 1961).

H. Chatterjee, Studies in Some Aspects of Hindu Saṃskāras in Ancient India (Calcutta, 1965).

K. V. Rangaswami Aiyangar, 'Dharmaśāstra in S. India with special reference to the contribution made by Sri Vedanta Deśika', J. As. Soc. Bombay 31-32 (1956/7), 5-19.

W. Ruben, Die gesellschaftliche Entwicklung im alten Indien: 1. Die Entwicklung der Produktionsverhältnisse (Berlin, 1967); 2. Die Entwicklung von Staat und Recht (Berlin, 1968).

J. D. M. Derrett, Religion, Law and the State in India (London, 1968).

K. R. R. Sastry, 'Hinduism and international law', Recueil des Cours (Académie de Droit International), 1966, I (vol. 117) (Leiden, 1967), 503-615 (see Derrett, IYBIA, 15-16, 1966-7, 328-47).

R. Lingat, The Classical Law of India (Berkeley, Univ. of Cal. Press, 1973).

H. Chatterjee, Śāstrī, The Law of Debt in Ancient India (Calcutta, 1971).
B. Guru Rajah Rao, Ancient Hindu Judicature (Madras, 1920).
S. Varadachariar, The Hindu Judicial System (Lucknow, 1949).

Caste

J. H. Hutton, Caste in India[2] (Bombay, 1951).
E. R. Leach, ed., Aspects of Caste in South India, Ceylon, and North-West Pakistan (Cambridge, 1962).
L. Dumont, Homo hierarchicus (Paris, 1967).
G. S. Ghurye, Caste and Race in India[5] (Bombay, 1969).
D. G. Mandelbaum, Society in India (Berkeley, 1970).
C. Bouglé, Essays on the Caste System (Cambridge, 1971).

Arthaśāstra, Administration and Political Ideas

J. J. Meyer, Das altindische Buch vom Welt- und Staatsleben (Leipzig, 1926).
V. R. Dikshitar, Maurya Polity (Madras, 1932).
K. V. Rangaswami Aiyangar, Some Aspects of Ancient Indian Polity (Madras, 1935).
K. V. Rangaswami Aiyangar, Indian Cameralism (Adyar, 1949).
R. K. Gupta, Political Thought in the Smṛti Literature (Allahabad, n. d. (1952), printed c. 1970).
U. N. Ghoshal, A history of Indian Political Ideas (Bombay, 1959).
A. S. Altekar, State and Government in Ancient India[4] (Delhi, 1962).
V. P. Varma, Studies in Hindu Political Thought[2] (Benares, 1959).
R. P. Kangle, The Kauṭilīya Arthaśāstra, 3 vols. (Bombay, 1960-5).
J. W. Spellman, Political Theory of Ancient India (Oxford, 1964).
G. S. Dikshit, Local Self-Government in Mediaeval Karṇāṭaka (Dharwar, 1964).
D. C. Sircar, Studies in the Society and Administration of Ancient and Medieval India, I (Calcutta, 1967).
B. N. Puri, History of Indian Administration I (Bombay, 1968).
H. Scharfe, Untersuchungen zur Staatsrechtslehre des Kauṭalya (Wiesbaden, 1968).
D. C. Sircar, Landlordism and Tenancy in Ancient and Medieval India (Lucknow, 1969).
J. D. M. Derrett, 'Rulers and ruled in India', Recueils Soc. Jean Bodin XXII (1969), 417-45.
T. R. Trautmann, Kauṭilya and the Arthaśāstra (Leiden, 1971).
Sachchidananda Sahai, 'Rājyaśāstra in ancient Cambodia', Vishveshvaranand Indological J. 9/1 (1971), 151-63.

Legal History

R. B. Pal, The History of Hindu Law in the Vedic Age (Calcutta, 1958).
P. L. Bhargava, India in the Vedic Age (Lucknow, 1971).
J. Gonda, The Vedic God Mitra (Leiden, 1972).
H. Cowell, History and Constitution of the Courts and Legislative Authorities in India[6] (Calcutta, 1936).
G. C. Rankin, Background to Indian Law (Cambridge, 1946).
U. C. Sarkar, Spochs of Hindu Legal History (Hoshiarpur, 1958).
T. K. Banerjee, Background to Indian Criminal Law (Calcutta, 1963).
V. Ramaswami, 'Hindu law and English judges', in V. V. Deshpande, ed., Studies in Law (Bombay, 1961). 319-29.
B. B. Misra, The Judicial Administration of the East India Company in Bengal, 1765-1782 (Delhi, 1961).

B. N. Pandey, The Introduction of English Law into India (London, 1967).
M. C. Setalvad, Role of English Law in India (Jerusalem, 1966).
H. P. Dubey, A Short History of the Judicial Systems of India ... (Bombay, 1968).
L. Rocher, 'Jacob Mossel's Treatise on the Customary Law of the Vellālar Chettiyars', JAOS, 89/1 (1969), 27-50.
M. P. Jain, Outlines of Indian Legal History[3] (Bombay, 1972).

Indian Law

J. Jolly, Outlines of a History of the Law of Partition, Inheritance and Adoption (Calcutta, 1885).
S. Roy, Customs and Customary Law in British India (Calcutta, 1911).
B. K. Acharyya, Codification in British India (Calcutta, 1914).
M. C. Setalvad, Common Law in India (London, 1960).
D. E. Smith, India as a Secular State (Princeton, 1963).
A. Gledhill, The British Commonwealth ... India[2] (London, 1964).
G. Austin, The Indian Constitution: Cornerstone of a Nation (Oxford, 1966).
G. S. Sharma, ed., Secularism: its Implications for Law and Life in India (Bombay, 1966).
D. C. Buxbaum, ed., Family Law and Customary Law in Asia (The Hague, 1968) (see T. Rama Rao at IYBIA, 15-16, 1966-7 (1970), 669-72.
P. B. Gajendragadkar, Secularism and the Constitution of India (Bombay, 1971).
J. M. Shelat, Secularism (Bombay, 1972).
V. R. Krishna Iyer, Law and the People (New Delhi, 1972).

Anglo- and Modern Hindu Law

W. Stokes, Hindu Law Books (Madras, 1865).
S. Setlur, A Complete Collection of Hindu Law Books on Inheritance (Madras, 1911).
B. D. Sirvya, Hindu Woman's Estate (Calcutta, 1913).
R. Sarvadhikari, The Principles of the Hindu Law of Inheritance[2] (Madras, 1922).
G. D. Banerjee, The Hindu Law of Marriage and Stridhana[5] (Calcutta, 1923).
B. C. Law, The Law of Gift in British India[2] (Calcutta, 1926).
J. L. Kapur, The Law of Adoption in India and Burma (Calcutta, 1933).
S. C. Bagchi, Juristic Personality of Hindu Deities (Calcutta, 1933).
J. R. Gharpure, Rights of Women under the Hindu Law (Bombay, 1943).
J. D. Mayne, Treatise on Hindu Law and Usage[11] (Madras, 1953).
J. D. M. Derrett, Introduction to Modern Hindu Law (Bombay, 1963).
D. F. Mulla, Principles of Hindu Law[13] (Bombay, 1966).
N. R. Raghavachariar, Hindu Law, Principles and Precedents[6] (Madras, 1972).
* M. N. Srinivasan, Principles of Hindu Law[4] (Allahabad, 1970).
R. L. Chaudhary, Hindu Women's Right to Property (Calcutta, 1961).
B. K. Mukherjea, Hindu Law of Religious and Charitable Trust[3] (Calcutta, 1970).
P. K. Virdi, The Grounds for Divorce in Hindu and English Law (a Study in Comparative Law) (Delhi, 1972).

---

* This work, in three volumes, somewhat hastily prepared and printed, is nevertheless the richest compilation of Hindu Law in its smallest details, with equal emphasis on the Anglo-Hindu law and the enactments of 1955-6.